PIRATES OF THE AIR

The Story of Radio Free Scotland

GORDON WILSON

Scots Independent (Newspapers) Ltd.

Published by
Scots Independent (Newspapers) Ltd
51 Cowane Street
Stirling FK8 1JW
Scotland
www.scotsindependent.org

ISBN: 978-0-9512820-8-3

Printed by Winter & Simpson
Tel: (01382) 813813

CONTENTS

DEDICATION AND THANKS

While for the most part, the breakthrough of the Scottish National Party was an exercise in dogged hard work, Radio Free Scotland brought a new dimension of romanticism to the movement. It was, of course, as it always would be a gesture – even in its illegality! Nonetheless, it illuminated the struggle for broadcasting justice – not yet fully secured – and gave hope to a movement when it was dispirited through lack of success.

So, a great deal of thanks are due to the pioneer David Rollo and his team in the 50s, those who recreated the station in Edinburgh in the 60s, Louis Stevenson, Frank Thomson and many others and the political dimension offered by Angus McIntosh and his associates in Glasgow in the sixties and early seventies.

The list of those who worked with stamina, inspiration, recklessness – and yes, much fun - is too great to carry here. And, indeed, the operators found it necessary to work anonymously to avoid capture. To all of them, the modern serious minded, conventional SNP owes a vote of gratitude.

Thanks must also be given to those who helped compile this history: David Rollo, Junior, Gerry Bayne, Eric Denovan, Ian Douglas, Ian Hamilton, Robin MacCormick, Sheila McIntosh, David Murchie and David Stevenson. Once again, I am indebted to Angus Lyon for his proof reading and to the SI team for their back-up.

With one exception, it has not proved possible to trace archived press photographs. These exist in clipping form only.

I dedicate this story to my wife, Edith whose first date with me was to an Edinburgh transmission and who has been my support throughout.

PIRATES OF THE AIR

Chapter 1

Launching the Station

Riding high on the crest of being the Government of Scotland, the Scottish National Party crashed into a familiar barrier during the Westminster General Election of May 2010. It was the barrier of broadcasting coverage and a reminder that in the eyes of London, Scotland was a region that deserved little special recognition. Over previous general elections, the electoral strength of the SNP in Scottish Parliament contests had enabled the Party to gain a respectable share of coverage, even when, at times, it struggled to make a relevant Scottish case amidst the welter of UK (and English) issues that invariably dominated Westminster.

For the first time, the UK moved over to a thinly disguised presidential system when the UK parties and the UK broadcasters (the BBC, ITV and Sky) offered to mount televised debates amongst the three UK political leaders. This left the SNP, Plaid Cymru and the Northern Ireland parties beached on their provincial shores and visibly detached from the campaigns run from London.

Naturally, the SNP and others protested. It was wrong for democracy, they said, that significant political forces in their own right should be deprived of fair coverage. They were just as much part of the United Kingdom as England. There were laws that governed the contesting of individual constituencies. Why should not similar rules be applied to the digital media?

Then again, it was not as if the leaders of the Conservative, Labour and the Liberal Democrats would be confined to the great affairs of the British state such as the economy, foreign affairs and defence.

The broadcasters conceded that to sustain the interest of the most populous nation of the United Kingdom, English domestic issues such as education, local government, transport and health must be discussed by the British leaders. It would only cause confusion, ran the argument, if provincial matters affecting Scotland, Wales and Northern Ireland and administered by their own parliaments, were introduced.

Of course, in a sophisticated democracy, sweeteners such as debates between local leaders carefully hidden from England were on offer – and reluctantly accepted. For the third time in its history, the SNP went to law by raising an action for judicial review and for the third time it lost. As in 1987 (when it was my decision as National Convener), it was a mistake. In an election campaign, if you fail to win you lose momentum. Given the Unionist tendencies of the Scottish Bench, the auguries were not good.

But in May 2010, the initial impact of the first televised debates was huge. Nick Clegg stole the show for the Liberal Democrats in the first programme, eclipsing Prime Minister Gordon Brown and his Conservative challenger, David Cameron. For a period the Lib/Dems dominated the scene until sanity prevailed.

It did not matter to the SNP that by the end of the election, Clegg and co. had lost ground in votes and seats. By then, the SNP campaign had been torpedoed. The Scottish themes had vanished from sight and with them the hope that the Party would make ground at Westminster. Most observers were of the view that had the SNP leader, Alex Salmond, taken part he would have destroyed the unionist parties over the danger to the economy from the massive debt overhang and the resultant savage cuts in public expenditure.

The 2010 election revealed that the nationalist parties faced ongoing institutional prejudice. It was not new, merely an important battle in a war that had its roots back at the beginnings of time – or at least until Scottish politics intruded on the Westminster preserves from 1960 onwards! Before then, the situation was worse.

In the 1950s, the nationalist movement in Scotland was in the doldrums. The SNP had met with two serious splits in the 40s – and encountered another in 1955. This left it enfeebled, although for the first time under a unified leadership. Still the largest body, the SNP shared the stage with Scottish National Congress, the remnants of the Scottish Covenant Association and the Scottish Patriots. Politically, Scotland fitted tightly in a unionist vice, with both the Conservative and Unionist Party (to give it its full title in Scotland) and the British Labour Party believing that Scotland would fare better under a centralised British structure of government. And it was the Conservatives who won a majority of the popular vote in 1955, with the two main parties each having 35 seats.

Yet things in broadcasting were about to change. It is worth remembering that television was a BBC monopoly until the mid fifties when Independent Television was established with regional companies providing local and UK competition to the BBC. In Scotland, the two new channels were Scottish Television (STV) covering the central belt and Grampian TV (with eastern, northeastern and northern Scotland as its franchised fiefdom). There was also Border TV which straddled the Scottish and English Borders (and had its headquarters in

Carlisle). BBC Radio was a monopoly, challenged only by Radio Luxembourg which most young people preferred to the very staid output of the BBC. In the wings – or rather to be moored out to sea beyond English territorial waters - was the 'pirate' commercial station, Radio Caroline, although this did not commence broadcasting until 1964.

In Scotland, a land-borne broadcasting insurrection took place. On 24 November 1956, Radio Free Scotland (RFS) was born. It was the first pirate radio station and its initial foray made banner headlines in the Scottish Sunday Express the following day. In its front page coverage, the Express gave its account of the broadcast:

"SCOTS TV SENSATION

All-night hunt for Mystery Station

SCOTTISH NATIONALISTS burst into TV – on sound last night, and in a 20-minute "pirate" broadcast told viewers: "The fight for independence is on in earnest"

They announced that other broadcasts would follow – saying: "This is the only way we can reach Scotland" – and appealed for fighting funds.

The broadcast appears to have been heard only in the Perth area. It was not heard in Edinburgh, Glasgow and Dundee. Experts said later the illegal transmitter – possibly small enough to operate from a van or car had been based in the Perth or North Fife area. And early this morning a nation-wide hunt was beginning for Britain's first radio gate-crashers who, with their technicians, may be liable to jail sentences.

There appeared to be four or five men and two women in the broadcast which came as the night's TV programme was ending.

Don't Switch Off

As viewers in Central Scotland prepared to switch off for the night they heard a man's voice cut into the news broadcast. Over a high pitched screech it said: "Attention, attention, this is Radio Free Scotland calling. Do not switch off. Listen when the BBC is off the air.

The weather forecast ended. The announcer smiled good night and after "The Queen", the screens went blank. Then accordions broke into the marching tune, "Scotland the Brave". An excited voice said: "This is Radio Free Scotland bringing to you the truth about the Home Rule Movement." It went on: "Nationalism has been banned from the air by the London controlled BBC." A second voice broke in: "No party contesting fewer than 100 seats is permitted to make broadcasts.

First voice: "There are only 71 seats in the whole of Scotland. The ban is complete." Said the excited voice: "But nationalism is thriving. Nationalism is spreading."

Gong Struck

A gong was struck and money jingled. – Scottish money said the voice, pouring into England at £500 million a year. Four more voices joined in, punctuated by the striking of a gong. They spoke of attempts to close down Clyde steamer services and branch railways. Back came the music and the announcer said loudly: "This is Radio Free Scotland proclaiming to the nation that the fight is on in earnest." The programme finished with "Scots Wha Hae." BBC engineers were last night trying to pin-point where the broadcast was coming from.

Urgent Calls

From Glasgow went urgent messages to BBC staff men at Kirk o' Shotts TV transmitting station and to Edinburgh engineers: "Try to fix this broadcast. Find out if you can monitor it."

But Scottish BBC chief Mr. Melville Dinwiddie said: "My publicity officer investigates reports of such matters. The publicity officer, Mr. Douglas Stewart *[who on retirement became an active member of the SNP]* said: "I have checked with Glasgow, Edinburgh and Meldrum in Aberdeenshire. Our people there did hear something, but it was not recognisable as speech."

Mr. Terence McInnes, of Arden Street, Maryhill, Glasgow, who heard the "rebel broadcast" in the lounge of a Perth hotel said later:

"It was really surprising. The people certainly put up a case. Whether they are right or wrong it was a bold piece of work. Everything came through quite clearly. Nobody here could think what was happening when it began."

A Perth police official said: "We did not hear this ourselves, but one of the people rang up to complain about it." Many viewers telephoned the Post Office to find out what was happening."

Sensational, yes, but a well-written piece, obviously offered as an exclusive to a mass-readership paper!

More reminiscent of a modern tabloid style was a follow-up article in the Sunday Express giving a sexy aura of mystery to RFS:

"Rendezvous with a Mystery Voice

Sylvia says – I'm the pirate radio girl

A HUSKY-VOICED girl spoke in a dingy café last night of her part in the "pirate" broadcasts of the Scottish nationalists. And she declared: "We really have little fear of being caught. Do I realise that I could be jailed? Of course……. We all knew before we started this."

Not her name

Three times in a week – first at Perth and twice at Kilmarnock – the "pirates" calling themselves "Radio Free Scotland", have crashed the BBC's television wavelength. Each time they have opened with the march "Scotland the Brave," following up with the nationalist propaganda. The girl I met in the café said that I might call her Sylvia – because that is not her real name. She said that she had taken part in all three broadcasts, and was now the only woman in the "Free Scotland" team. Another woman took part in the first broadcast. But Sylvia said: "Her voice seemed to be recognised by other nationalists in Perth and we decided to take no chances of a sympathiser inadvertently giving her away."

Enough petrol

"One of the men was recognised too, and he had to drop out. Because there are so few of us each person has an allotted task in addition to taking part in the broadcasts. My job is to arrange petrol supplies. (*note: this was shortly after the British/French invasion of the Suez Canal had threatened to jeopardise supplies*). Now I think I have ensured we shall have as much petrol to take us to all the towns we intend to visit." Which towns....? Sylvia smiled - but said nothing. She drew on her gloves, walked from the café – and vanished into the night."

Other papers also covered the early days of Radio Free Scotland. For example the Daily Mail on 10 December 1956 gave an account of intense activity on the part of RFS in its first manifestation.

"SCOTS RADIO PIRATES CUT IN AT TEA-TIME

The Scottish Nationalist radio pirates changed their tactics last night. They broke into the BBC's television wavelength five hours earlier than usual. Kilmarnock viewers heard the call sign for the fourth time in a fortnight. The broadcasts are normally at the end of the London transmissions (*note: then around or just after 11pm*). But last night the mystery voice came on the air immediately after a religious broadcast and at the beginning of a 55-minute interval which began at 6.5pm.

Scottish Dance Music

On November 26 Kilmarnock viewers heard the pirates at 6 o'clock in the evening – but only for a few minutes. A call sign was broadcast, but there was no commentary until the BBC closed down. Four days later the second programme was heard in Kilmarnock, Irvine and Kilwinning and the other two broadcasts on December 3 and December 9 were also heard on the West Coast. Last night for 12 minutes, a man and a woman broadcast a commentary backed by Scottish dance music tunes."

CHAPTER 2

The Hunt

After 55 years, it is not surprising that there is little oral testimony of what happened from those who took the risks. The great flood of time has borne most away and with them the identity of the operators. I have no idea who "Sylvia" was. What is known is that Radio Free Scotland was the brain child of David Rollo, then Treasurer of the Scottish National Party who, with his languid manner, was a lateral thinker, well capable of putting his flights of fancy into practice. David Rollo was an amateur radio "ham" who had the technical ability to construct a transmitter – not that he would need to draw much upon his great expertise as a consultant electrical engineer! He died several years ago, leaving no records of his activities, but was of the view that the creation of RFS was his greatest political achievement. Then, and later, in the SNP, he took a great interest in "legitimate" broadcasting matters as they affected Scotland and drew up a submission to the Pilkington Commission on Broadcasting on behalf of the Party.

According to David's son, also David, the transmitter was constructed in the back shop of Alvaro Rossi's Townhead Café in Kirkintilloch. Both Alvaro and David were registered "hams". The café was not used as a transmission site.

One witness to the impact made by RFS comes from me. In the autumn of 1956, I was a first year law student at the University of Edinburgh and a new member of the University Nationalist Club Like my fellow members, I was still excited after the success of the Club in organising one of the biggest political demonstrations since the thirties. The demonstration over the soon to be abortive British/French invasion of the Suez Canal split the campus. On the side of righteousness – and international order - stood the combined forces of the nationalist and left wing political clubs, cultural societies and students from the Commonwealth and Colonies – backed up I have to say by the muscle of the boxing and judo clubs. On the imperial side were the Conservatives, medical students and the rugby club. Having been the only student identified in an Express photo as a participant in a demonstration banned by the University, my student days might have been numbered.

None of the members of the Nationalist Club had any illusions about the political situation. We were all aware of the dreadful straits of the movement. There was not much hope around, even for young idealists. The ethos of EUNC was different from home rule clubs in other universities. The Edinburgh Club designated itself as "nationalist" rather than "national" and was little involved in student politics or debating. Its tendency was more towards revolution than devolution – an attitude that was adopted by students worldwide only ten years later.

So when Radio Free Scotland burst on to the air, the significant publicity generated was a boost to confidence. We sensed a way ahead for the national movement despite its fissures and electoral failures, perhaps even by way of unorthodox political methods.

Students were not alone in this. There are clippings of photographs of BBC broadcasting vans being decorated. And at a time when a Facebook Wall did not exist, it was a wall of St Andrews House, the home of the Scottish civil service, which was whitewashed. Radio Free Scotland obviously filled a gap at a time when there was little political effort, and the political landscape was bare of any trace of significant publicity for the nationalist cause. The slogan was not original nor the lettering artistic. It read: "Listen to Radio Free Scotland!"

This was not easy to do as RFS seemingly visited Scotland's capital once only and was active elsewhere. Certainly, the publicity continued. "Sylvia" did not make another appearance. But Bobby MacLeod, the celebrated accordionist and Scottish Country Dance Band leader offered to play with his band on Radio Free Scotland. In a report, the 31 year old band leader said that during a series of one night stands throughout the country people kept asking him: "Why don't you broadcast for the Nationalists?" He did not think the offer would interfere with any regular TV or radio appearances – the band had made about 60 broadcasts over an 8 year period since they had been formed.

A rather more bizarre notion appeared in another undated clipping from the Reynolds News (like many other journals long laid to rest). Obviously shortly after the first broadcast, it carried a story from people unconnected with RFS, but riding with the publicity. It was interesting to see the viral spread from the first broadcast.

"Scots may buy time to 'plug' freedom

SCOTTISH NATIONALISTS, who startled televiewers with two pirate broadcasts last week, may continue to broadcast – without breaking the law. A new plan has been put forward since police and GPO engineers stepped up their hunt for the pirate transmitter. Spurred on by the interest the broadcasts have aroused, a group of Nationalists is planning to buy radio time to put across their views. Likely station for these broadcasts is Radio

Eireann, which carries sponsored programmes and is clearly received in Scotland.

The plan would also have the wider backing of the Nationalist movement than the present so-called "Radio Free Scotland" broadcasts which break the law. Buying time on Radio Eireann would cost no more than the present pirate transmitter in Scotland."

But this was an erratic deviation. The press followed up on the hunt for Radio Free Scotland. The Daily Mail after the first broadcast carried the headline: "**Hunt is on for Scots Pirate Radio**", claiming the apparatus could be in the boot of a car. It declared that GP detector vans had patrolled lonely hilly Scottish roads waiting for any further broadcasts. Police and radio experts were working on a theory that the pirate radio station had operated from a hill above Perth. Meanwhile, Scottish nationalist leaders of all groups had hailed the pirate broadcast as the biggest coup since the "Stone of Destiny" raid on Westminster Abbey. A GPO spokesman in London said: "It seems pretty clear that it was a radio transmission and not interference with the landline." After discussing the techniques of transmission and how detector vans worked (with the kind expression that this was how Third Columnists had been traced during the war!), the article concluded that penalties could range from fines of a few pounds to prison sentences of three months.

An unidentified newspaper followed up the story with a view that the Headquarters of the Radio might be in Glasgow and quoted a Chief Detective Superintendent of Glasgow Police, Peter MacGregor that he was taking a close interest in the "bandit" broadcast, even though it had taken place in Perth outside his area. The report went into the background of rumours of trial transmissions and after looking at the difficulties in pin-pointing a low powered set, came to the conclusion that the greatest danger to the pirates lay in loose talk.

And so the stories multiplied. The Pictorial had a banner headline of RFS extending into Edinburgh and on 11 December it was reported that the pirate radio had been heard for the first time in scattered areas of north Glasgow. The Sunday Dispatch carried a headline: "**Yard called in to trace TV Pirates**", explaining that Special Branch detectives had been called in to help GPO experts to track down the Radio Free Scotland transmitter, which had gate-crashed the BBC wavelength three times in a week. To add sauce to the tale, it was claimed that anonymous business men had offered cash to set up other illegal transmitters and the police were worried that the broadcasts could become seditious. One officer said: "So far these broadcasts have been fairly responsible, nationalist propaganda and so on, but nothing dangerous. But there are several nationalist groups who are more extreme, and the possibility is that they will try to inflame public opinion." Encouragement for the RFS operators came in a highlighted paragraph: "**Most Scottish viewers are keeping their sets switched on after the BBC closedown – to see if we can hear the pirates.**"

And just to show that there were real dangers from loose talk and even looser print, a story emanating from Edinburgh carried the message: "A radio engineer member of the party employed by one of the city's biggest electrical firms is making it in his flat. Two graduates in electrical engineering from Edinburgh University are helping him." Obviously the source forgot that if the GPO wished to trace a transmitter, the easiest way was to follow the man they had tagged! The only consolation was that this loose talk did not come from Radio Free Scotland.

Chapter 3

The End Game?

While most of the nationalist leaders applauded RFS, a more cautious response came from Dr. Robert McIntyre, Chairman of the SNP who, in an initial statement, said he had no official knowledge of the pirate broadcasts – the phrasing suggesting he knew of them unofficially. But he did say that the Party executive would be discussing them and the SNP's attitude towards them at their next meeting. More significantly in another report, he went so far as to say that no Scot should help in the hunt by the Post Office to track down the broadcasters and that he would continue to support them so long as they remained responsible, pointing out that there was nothing immoral in it because the BBC had abused their monopoly.

Very soon the SNP, the largest body in the then splintered national movement, swung behind Radio Free Scotland. The Scots Independent, associated with the SNP, but not controlled by it, zeroed in on the reasons why the pirate radio had commenced operations. So far press publicity had naturally concentrated on the illicit nature of the broadcasts, the GPO hunt and which areas had been covered by the transmissions. Now, for the first time, the reasons were given.

In its edition of 1 December 1956, in a front page article, the Scots Independent dwelt on the political situation. It made clear that the two London Parties had banned all Scottish political broadcasts. Facts about the economic situation and the burden of the incorporating Union were now being broadcast, along with demolition of myths about the Home Rule movement.

The caution of the first response had gone. Now there was a call that no Scotsman or woman, worthy of the name, in whatever capacity employed, should assist officialdom in its efforts to pursue and track down the nationalist broadcasters. The moral case was asserted. There was to be no mistake. Freedom of speech was at risk if this radio was suppressed. It was evident, ran the report that the then Conservative Government and the Labour opposition had gone out of their way to preserve their political monopoly on the air.

"They have abused the power of government to protect their interests. This time they have gone too far. Their action in modern times is equivalent to suppression of a free press."

While the national movement had often been harmed by stunts of one kind or another, Radio Free Scotland was not just a stunt. It was a bold attempt to break the radio ban on reasonable freedom of speech on the air. The broadcast was handled very well and those who heard it all state that the speakers knew what they were talking about."

Fourteen days later, the National Council of the SNP gave its unanimous support. To make sure the matter was dealt with, Radio Free Scotland had written to the SNP. It set out three reasons why RFS merited the support of the Party:

1.   We do not agree in principle with the establishment of unauthorised Broadcasting Stations by individuals or groups of individuals

without very good moral grounds. By the Government's action in banning political discussion by Scottish and Welsh parties, they have forced us to take this action to vindicate the rights of free speech on the air.

2.   Nevertheless we realise the danger which could arise if our transmissions were not regulated in some way by a responsible body representing Scottish political opinion, and therefore have approached the only Scottish Political Party.

3.   On our part we would be agreeable to any reasonable control by your Party over the political content of our broadcasts.

The letter ended with the request that arrangements be made which will let the public know that these transmissions are carried on in a responsible manner and with the approval of the Party.

With the backing of the SNP and receipt of a telegram of congratulations from Plaid Cymru, the way was set fair for RFS to thrive. The next set of broadcasts was directed to Perth, Glasgow and Kilmarnock. In a short programme of news, RFS covered rising unemployment, sponsored emigration, civil aviation and Prestwick. In a series of points, a spokesman outlined Scotland's exporting efforts by illustrating the high earnings that flowed into the London Treasury from engineering, shipping, textiles, food production and the whisky trade. The programme concluded with the interview with "Mr John Mackay" about self-government policy.

By the end of December, the issues covered in Stirlingshire included the radio ban, the tax on shale oil and emigration. The topic of emigration came up frequently. Then, and over the next fifteen years, Scotland lost its life blood as young families gave up hope of a better life and "upped-sticks" and went to settle in the Commonwealth, mainly in Canada, Australia and New Zealand where in many cases, folk had relatives who had settled earlier. At the time, Australia ran a scheme where sponsored emigrants were given a boat passage (too early for air travel!) on a one way ticket at the cost of £10. This, and earlier migration, is one reason why the population of Scotland remained static while that of England rose dramatically. It was very much a rubbed sore for those who stayed behind.

So it was not surprising that RFS directed attention to the scandalous city slums and the need for income to get a decent home. Again and again it concentrated on the need to modernise Scottish industry and upgrade the roads and railways.

Support for RFS was expressed in practical ways. Oliver Brown, a distinguished nationalist, expecting that the radio operators and others would be caught and tried, volunteered to contribute towards the income of families whose breadwinners had been incarcerated – a little reminder, perhaps, that it was not a prank.

By February, 1957, the furore had died down. RFS had made 30 broadcasts in many areas of central Scotland. Now the Radio was asking people who were paying the radio licence of £3 to send a similar contribution to RFS at the Glasgow headquarters of the SNP. There was a plaintive tone implicit in a challenge to the press to give it coverage as now little mention of activities had appeared in the national papers. Indeed, in Edinburgh, we did not know that RFS had continued to broadcast beyond the first splash of publicity. Only the Scots Independent continued to give news of its activities. The bright spot was that the transmitters were more powerful and reception, always a bug-bear, had become much clearer.

Still Radio Free Scotland persevered. It covered the May Conference of the SNP and had a panel chaired by Arthur Donaldson, a future leader of the Party and composed of Gwynfor Evans, President of Plaid Cymru and SNP Chairman James Halliday. This was likely to be the very first time there had been a broadcast from an SNP Conference, whose proceedings were studiously ignored by the state broadcasters. Such was the drought of coverage that when news of the broadcast broke, SNP members at a social in the Station Hotel, Perth, rushed to the television room to hear the discussion.

Not all of the broadcasts were ignored. In June, the Dundee Courier advanced the theory under bold headlines that poor television coverage in Perth (for which the BBC had already given an apology!) had been caused by a pirate radio van operating on behalf of the Home Rule movement! A letter of protest ended up with a reference at the bottom of an obscure column with no title and containing various snippets of news. RFS was probably lucky even to get that obscure correction!

Dr. Eric Denovan, then a Dundee GP, has described a false alarm when his house was used as a transmission site:

> "They then rigged an aerial from our chimney to a telegraph pole in our garden and found the area was good. We next recorded a programme on tape and arranged a date to broadcast. The transmitter was set up in a room with a window out to the garden. Fortunately we had a high wall as our next-door neighbour was a retired police Inspector. All went well until a car stopped outside our house and two men In long raincoats and soft hats got out and rang our door-bell. While I went to answer the door, feeling decidedly nervous, the

transmitter and crew made a rapid exit through the window. Fortunately our visitors were David Rollo and son."

David, Junior has recounted one memorable broadcast inspired by an article by John Gordon of the Sunday Express who had argued that the UK Parliament should be transferred to Edinburgh. Radio Free Scotland did a "spoof" news bulletin that might have been broadcast in that event. It ranged from a blow by blow commentary on the World Shinty Test Match series to the Crown Jewels being stolen from Edinburgh Castle and the police draining Hogganfield Loch, near Glasgow as the result of a tip off.

From then on, Radio Free Scotland largely disappeared from sight. The Scots Independent of 15 October 1957 carried a heavyweight script on The Nation and the Family and shortly after there was a report that the Radio had moved into the southern counties but had been defeated by the terrain of the Highlands and North East. It had two transmitters in use. Glasgow was the location in February 1958 and Dundee in May.

In November 1958, RFS had provided a transmitter for Wales. Radio Wales made its first transmission a month later. The last recorded broadcast of the first phase of Radio Free Scotland occurred in Hamilton during the General Election when the SNP candidate, David Rollo, the creator of RFS, fittingly made an election broadcast. Despite having printed some supervening scripts, the Scots Independent intriguingly introduced its report by saying that the last broadcast had been heard two years before. The proper conclusion is that RFS had gradually fizzled out, with perhaps isolated transmissions being made from time to time. It seemed the end of "ane auld sang".

Chapter 4

The Tartan Pimpernels Reappear

From 1956 onwards, the media had lost interest in the pirate radio once the novelty factor had faded. For people living in the east, there had been little chance of us hearing any of the broadcasts. But the impact of Radio Free Scotland had not vanished completely.

Then, from inside the membership of Edinburgh University Nationalist Club came new leadership. The co-founders were Louis Stevenson and myself. Both of us were in our final law degree year and near to concluding our third year of apprenticeship as solicitors. Louis Stevenson was to build a transmitter and deal with the technical aspects. I assumed the job of preparing the programmes. The transmitter was hand-made and as it was not properly protected by a metal case it was unreliable if knocked in transit. Getting it to work reliably and consistently was no easy task. It also needed a crystal cut specially in the United States to match the frequency of BBC TV in Scotland.

This was only part of the preparations. We had to get several teams together to prepare the programmes, transmit them and look after publicity. As the station was illegal, the transmission teams were to be kept separate from the other operations. On the programme side, despite having no experience of broadcasting or journalism, I was looking for people with an ability to write and edit, a facility with speech and above all, reliability. As nationalists were in short supply at this time, recruitment was difficult. Publicity was also vital if RFS were to attract any worthwhile listening public.

Without the benefit of the operating problems experienced by the 1956 station that we had assumed was long dead, we decided – helped no doubt by a lack of transport (law apprentices were paid around £100 a year and cars were a rare luxury) – to confine our operation to Edinburgh and its environs. Our aim was to build up a core audience and to broadcast at the same time every week so that people would know when to tune in.

It was obvious that publicity would be the life blood of the new Radio Free Scotland so that people would learn of our existence and join that proposed audience. Here we were fortunate to find a Public Relations Officer who would fit the spirit of the enterprise. The publicity side was to be filled with distinction by Frank Thomson, who would pelt the Press with letters and press releases. Louis Stevenson recruited nationalists who worked in the electronics factory at Ferranti to look after the engineering side before - inconveniently for me and the others, that is – marrying an American student and moving to Chicago in 1960, leaving me by default in sole charge. It also posed a technical problem. Louis Stevenson had built the transmitter and knew its frailties better than anyone else.

There were trial programmes and broadcasts before the first publicised transmission took place on 11 March 1960. In Edinburgh, at any given time, staffing would come from a pool of 15 people. RFS was intended to transmit weekly for eight months in the year so stamina was needed. The operating crew functioned as a cell on its own. Apart from me, Frank Thomson was the public face of RFS.

From the start, it was agreed that irreverence was the element that would attract the attention of the media and the public, so Frank Thomson and I held a press conference at the Edinburgh Branch SNP rooms at 16 North St Andrew Street to launch the station. There was a small turn out of journalists – after all this was a return – not a premiere. But they came and we were not unhappy with the response and there was news coverage in the Edinburgh evening papers, the Scotsman, the Express and Mail. The Daily Express was attracted to the new look programmes, drawing attention under the headline: **"Pirate Pops are Here"** and mentioning, after dismissing the news content rather hurtfully as "nationalist propaganda", that the new station included a disc spot entitled "Pirate Pops" dedicated to well known personalities.

The largest piece appeared in the Daily Mail.

"Challenge by a Radio Pirate

A YOUNG lawyer who is prepared to defend himself in court cut in on the BBC wavelength in Scotland last night and broadcast from a new "pirate" radio station. As he listened to his "taped" voice, the lawyer, 22-year old Gordon Wilson of Edinburgh, said: "Technically this station is illegal but if the police act I'll fight it in court." The broadcast started a minute after BBC TV closed down, and lasted 17 minutes. Three other men and two women broadcast with Mr. Wilson.

Liberty

The station - Radio Free Scotland – will transmit every Thursday night at 11.11pm. on the BBC wavelength. The programme was heard in parts of Edinburgh, Portobello and Fife towns. It was introduced by Edinburgh City Pipe Band playing "Scotland the Brave".....recorded of course.

And Mr. Wilson began by emphasising: "We do not consider what we are doing is against the law. We declare that any law which detracts from the liberty of citizens of one of the most ancient and respected European nations from making their views known to fellow country men and women is illegal itself." The "pirates" – they are 15 strong – refuse to recognise "the present undemocratic and repressive prohibition on Scottish political broadcasts.

They want a national Government and Parliament for Scotland. They also dedicated a record to the Scottish Secretary, Mr. John McLay. It was Elvis Presley, singing "Hound Dog", containing the line: *"You ain't nothin' but a rabbit, and you ain't no friend of mine"."*

This publicity triggered a number of feature articles. The Bulletin ran an account with a photograph of the programme makers, two girls and me, recording a future show. The Evening Dispatch ran a longer piece under the heading, "**Edinburgh – After Dark**" and having listened in, indicated that the first effort was clearly audible although fluctuating in volume. There was the usual tabloid response to the first programme – "**GPO Men to Hunt Channel 3 Pirates**" quoting the resolve of the GPO to track down the rebels as "they do not have a transmitting licence."

Ever anxious to keep a good story rolling, I added my tuppence worth: "We know how efficient these engineers can be if they put their minds to it. But our own boys can get off the mark fairly quickly too. It should be quite exciting."

Robin MacCormick, another nationalist student lawyer – and Edinburgh University seemed to breed them then – tells of his connection with RFS as a member of Edinburgh University Nationalist Club.

"I recollect gatherings in Gordon Wilson's flat (long since demolished) in Fountainbridge where plans were made for the content of the broadcasts and for suitable broadcasting locations. On one warm summer evening, so warm that the window in Gordon's sitting room was open, he was directing us what needed to be done. In my case, I had to write a short piece about the high rate of emigration from Scotland caused by the parlous economic condition of the country and I believe that I did indeed record the piece for broadcasting. I remember comparing the emigration rate to the disappearance every year of the entire population of Inverness, capital of the Highlands. Equally memorable was the suggestion that, with Gordon's clear and resounding voice, he hardly needed a radio transmitter to broadcast his message to the people of Edinburgh, just the open window.

Possibly during the same summer, I volunteered to provide a spot for making a broadcast – namely the attic of my parents' two-storey home in the Grange district to the South of Edinburgh. It was not particularly high up and lay on a south-facing slope covering the suburbs, rather than the populous city centre. But, my parents being away on holiday, it was available.

We lugged the heavy equipment up the stairs and then up a ladder into the roomy attic in time for the end of the day's TV programming and the broadcast went out as planned. However, as it neared the end, the monitor which kept tabs on the officials who were trying to trace the source told us that their little van was not far away in a neighbouring street. We all heaved a sigh of relief when we were able to switch off the transmitter well before our location could be identified."

Much thought had gone into the shape of the programmes so as to make the politics palatable to casual listeners.

The first programme had a magazine format. It consisted of the following items:-

Introductory music		Scotland the Brave
Statement of Aims and Ideals		Gordon Wilson
News Items –	Unemployment	Jean Montgomery
	Roads	Gordon Wilson
	Housing	Gordon Wilson
	Emigration	Hamish Grant
	Round-up	Gordon Wilson
Music	Hound Dog	Elvis Presley
Legal & Moral Basis for Broadcasting		Hamish Grant
Music	The Dean of Westminster	Sandy Patton
Additional News Item		Louis Stevenson
Wind-up		

This edition was designed to set the scene and was more heavy-weight than others that followed. The team was not doing this for fun so there was substantial political coverage, lightened with music. BBC Radio, before the days of Radio Caroline, RFS's distinguished and more notorious competitor, was also heavy going. So, although there was more political content on RFS than modern tastes would permit, the efforts, although undeniably amateurish to begin with, were eminently 'listenable'. Peggy Phillips, the Radio and TV critic commented in the Scotsman on 15 July 1963:

> "BBC's Scotland in Parliament is a praiseworthy if slightly dreich attempt to keep us in touch with Westminster from a purely Scottish angle. Scotland's state being what it is, one hankers for a little more fire under the pot. Radio Free Scotland – off for the holidays, but immeasurably improved in reception and content at my last listening – had the notion in its *"The Week at Westminster"*.
>
> Without demanding quite as much, one feels the BBC's programme would be enlivened if the planners incorporated each time one awkward well-informed patriot, who puts Scotland before politics, and allowed him to ask one awkward well-informed question of the MPs present."

It seems preposterous, in these days of 'round the clock' TV coverage that BBC TV (there were no BBC2 or digital channels) went off air at some point between 10pm and 11.15pm. When the picture faded after God Save the Queen, the TV transmitters emitted what was called a carrier wave for 3 minutes. This occupied the frequency and blocked transmission. For the preliminary period, Radio Free Scotland, with its weak power output, needed to use distinctive music to penetrate the curtain. Initially, the station used a recording of Scotland the Brave by the Edinburgh Police pipe band. This started with a staccato drumbeat followed by the ether-rending sound of the pipes and the announcement: **"Radio Free Scotland. This is Radio Free Scotland calling."** The introduction was still too short and fairly soon, the programme added the Grand March from Aida, where the trumpets continued the task of attracting an audience.

Chapter 5

Keeping the Audience

As the 1956 station had found, obtaining early coverage and perpetuating it are two different things. For the first month, RFS rang the changes. While keeping up the "cops and robbers" theme – and green detector vans from all over the UK were patrolling Edinburgh - to maintain media interest, it also intervened in the political arena – something that the SNP did not do in Edinburgh. There was a by-election in North Edinburgh Constituency. The SNP did not have a candidate so, in the interests of public service, it offered to give all the candidates an opportunity to put their case before the electorate.

Of course, the station was sorry, but hardly surprised, when none of the candidates felt able to take part. Instead, using news clippings, they presented the candidates' views on the issues – and also put forward arguments that would have been deployed by a Home Rule candidate. They felt they had a notch on their scabbard when the Liberal candidate declared that he did not feel that it was right that any political party, no matter how small, should be prohibited from taking part in election broadcasts on the BBC.

Aside from the illegality, some trends were working for RFS. The output of the BBC had been incredibly staid for years. With independent television at last on screen, there was a new radio audience also available to be tapped. The illegal Radio Free Scotland was not alone. The huge market for pop music and advertising was not restricted to Radio Luxembourg broadcasting out of British jurisdiction. The prospect of advertising led to commercial pirate stations, such as Radio Caroline. But Radio Free Scotland and Radio Wales were unique. They were political and to keep in touch with demand also tried to be entertaining. The radio piracy went only so far to attract audiences. To keep them was the main challenge.

Fortunately, Radio Free Scotland was not strapped in the same corset as the BBC. It was free to experiment. In terms of production, discussion elements were restricted to not more than three or three and a half minutes. Interviews were preferred to monologues. The serious stuff was interspersed with music and the whole show was wrapped up in around twenty minutes. Not only was this a good length to sustain audience interest, any longer would have given the detector vans a better chance to triangulate the transmitter and pin it down.

As time passed, RFS production teams gained experience in writing, interviewing, editing and presenting. With the great benefit of this expertise, changes were made to the programmes. Pirate Pops became a request show (restricted only by a rather narrow range of records, but got round by asking for a dedicated request for a named person rather than for a particular record). Each week there would be a simple – very simple – quiz, offering a box of Duncans chocolates to the first three winners. This was a great draw and brought in a healthy number of answers – on one week, reaching 31 - which, we were told by one of the Edinburgh newspapers, evidenced a significant amount of audience participation. And every one was not a loser; they got a leaflet about RFS or joining the SNP.

To stop the response from flagging, RFS deployed its secret weapon – cheek. It sent a publicised call to the Queen, promising that Scotland would be loyal to the Crown, if the Crown were loyal to Scotland and recognised an independent Scotland. The Queen was, of course, invited to listen and a letter was delivered to Holyrood House, where she was in residence. The Chief Constable of Edinburgh Police was given the opportunity to use the services of RFS for road safety campaigns.

Since personalities also added zest, the Radio acquired a mobile tape recorder, then in its infancy and prohibitively expensive. The team was able to tape more interviews, mostly with nationalist leaders or representatives such as Robert McIntyre, Arthur Donaldson, James Halliday, Ian Macdonald, William Wolfe, Wendy Wood and Robert Blair Wilkie. Occasionally, there were interviews with personalities like Hugh McDiarmid. Themed programmes were produced also. One featuring Leith and the views of a local minister, James Marshall on care of the elderly, produced the interesting local phenomenon of sharply reducing the response from the audience in South Fife, for whom Leith, although just across the Firth of Forth, was a bridge or ferry too far!

The fragile nature of the transmitter built by Louis Stevenson was a major hurdle to progress. It had no protective casing and was always on the move. It had a distressing tendency to fail without warning. This did not help the Radio to build up a regular audience. It was also mortifying to the programme compilers to find that a show on which they had devoted hours of time was not transmitted. This happened with the well-publicised broadcast to the Queen who was at Holyroodhouse. It was even more distressing to hear later that the Duke of Edinburgh had tuned in fruitlessly! Thanks to Louis Stevenson, then in the USA, RFS procured a replacement Hallicrafter transmitter and in 1962, a more powerful model, the Viking Challenger. Both of these solved the twin problems of reliability and power.

Over a three year period, RFS obtained steady publicity in newspapers such as The Record, The Bulletin, Daily Herald, the Glasgow Herald, the Scotsman, Scottish Daily Express, Scottish Daily Mail, the Guardian, the Sunday Pictorial, the Observer, the Sunday Telegraph and other Scottish Sundays together with coverage in the Edinburgh Evening News and Edinburgh Evening Dispatch. Some of this publicity was in the form of feature articles. There were also news items and interviews on BBC radio and television and Scottish Television. Granada TV produced a 30 minute programme on Radio Wales, the Welsh counterpart of Radio Free Scotland. There was also an interview with Julian Pettifer on BBC Nationwide. The feature was not carried, but we had the extreme pleasure of receiving a BBC cheque for £35 (a large amount for those days) made out to Radio Free Scotland. As the Bank of Scotland had not turned a hair on our opening an account in name of Radio Free Scotland the cheque was quickly cashed. In all, RFS probably got more publicity than the SNP. This is as much a commentary on the profile of the SNP as on the lack of interest in independence amongst the media.

As a result, as the Radio expanded its base from Edinburgh to Glasgow and West Lothian, the mystique grew. Even today, a large number of nationalists, now getting on in years, will proudly admit to hosting the radio. These included Annie Knight, who was Scotland's oldest woman, when she died in 2006. Her living room was the scene of a broadcast in 1962.

So what was the real coverage? It was difficult to tell. Edinburgh was a very difficult area in which to secure overall reception. The hilly terrain did not suit VHF transmitters and there was usually around 60% coverage. This extended into southern and eastern Fife. Stray signals were picked up in coastal towns further to the north, such as Montrose. A survey was conducted in most parts of Edinburgh in August 1960. 910 people were interviewed, some in the street and some in their homes. The results showed:

80% of the sample had heard of Radio Free Scotland

13% had listened to the programmes.

90% of those who had listened to the programmes would continue to tune in.

80% of those who had not yet listened intended to do so.

75% of the sample was in favour of more control of Scots affairs by Scots and of Scotland having more say in governing herself.

Scottish Television made reference to the survey in their mid-day and evening newscasts. It was good to get recognition from another broadcasting organisation! In all, it was estimated that at one time or another 75,000 people had tuned in.

Over the next three years, Radio Free Scotland continued to broadcast in Edinburgh under my supervision as Director of Programmes. Apart from a four month break each summer, there was a regular 20-minute broadcast each week. It was hard work that left little time for relaxation and we were helped on the programming side by a reliable core, changing slightly over the years, as some emigrated or gravitated to other parts of Scotland. Edinburgh University Nationalist Club provided a good source of recruits on both a permanent and temporary basis. It was a fine form of training and in due course of time two members of staff - Douglas Henderson became a Westminster MP and Allan Macartney an MEP. As my flat mate, Roy MacIver, later Secretary General of COSLA and another lawyer, had little chance of escaping involvement.

The changes in personnel helped provide ideas although some weeks, we had to scratch our heads for inspiration as news stories seemed to have dried up. RFS came back in the late summer of 1960 with a special Festival edition featuring Robin Hall, the well known folk musician, Hugh MacDiarmid, Alex McCrindle, organiser of Equity in Scotland, Robert Garioch Sutherland, the poet and Jack O'Connor, a trade union organiser and an official in Glasgow Folk Song Society. It was a line up to be proud of. But the programme was jammed!

By mid-1963, my stewardship was drawing to a close when I took a job in Paisley. The restructuring meant that Douglas Henderson assumed the task of production as Director of Programmes. I became responsible for co-ordinating the three operating stations. As a joke and aping the BBC, I was given the title of General Controller. This might have gone to my head if there had been any money. Alas there was none!

CHAPTER 6

The Bridgeton Raid and Other Adventures

Running a pirate station was exhilarating. No one knew what was around the corner. Anecdotes abound. In its early days, RFS engineers kept a listening watch on the detector vans as they patrolled the streets attempting to locate the Scarlet Pimpernels of the Air, as one newspaper termed RFS. When one of the vans, from England - obviously unfamiliar with Edinburgh streets - turned into a cul-de-sac, RFS engineers sent a friendly message to the Post Office team on the PO frequency, suggesting they back out!

To raise funds, appeals were issued. One went to the Chairmen of the Scottish Banks. Excitement was tangible when I received an invitation from the then Earl of Airlie to call on him one lunchtime at the Head Office of the Royal Bank of Scotland. I was taken by messenger to the huge Directors' Room on the first floor. Lunch was out, but tea and biscuits were supplied and Lord Airlie was told, as we sat in arm chairs before a coal fire, what RFS was doing and why. It was a very pleasant conversation and very much above the pay-grade of a law apprentice. Although a pitch was made for money, sadly no bank draft for megabucks or even minibucks came through the mail afterwards. Nor was there a traditional, anonymous brown envelope stuffed with freshly printed Royal Bank of Scotland 'tenners'.

On another occasion, the public relations officer who took over from Frank Thomson discovered a discarded army medium wave transmitter amongst TA surplus and the Radio agreed that it would try to transmit on medium wave. This was not practical as the set would have required high power and a huge antenna draped over trees. On one Saturday morning, filled with ambition, I joined the engineers at our ground flat in Gorgie (condemned for human habitation as a house because a burn ran through it, but useful as a workshop and it only cost £75 to buy!). Up rolled an Army truck. A group of TA soldiers jumped down, under the command of a TA officer who was our PRO, and unloaded this huge radio which was over five feet high, and carried it into the workshop in sections. Now, that would have interested Special Branch, and not surprisingly the RFS PRO/TA officer kept his identity secret. The soldiers were well rewarded with beer money! But the medium range transmitter never functioned.

RFS came into its own during the Glasgow Bridgeton By-election (1961) and the West Lothian By-election (1962) when it was invited to prepare programmes featuring the SNP candidates, Ian Macdonald and William Wolfe. Publicity for these unofficial election broadcasts gave a dash of excitement to what emerged as significant electoral advances for the SNP.

The authorities made their move in Bridgeton. The broadcast had been widely announced and, of course, infringed both the statutory rules for election coverage and the Wireless Telegraphy Act. The GPO had it jammed. The GPO, which was responsible for enforcing broadcasting regulations and the Police who assisted them, identified the location of the transmission – a top flat tenanted by a Post Office employee!

On this occasion, the Edinburgh Branch of the Radio was carrying out the operation. For co-ordination, I was present at the transmission. For some weeks before, there had been a technical problem, transferring sound from the tape recorder to the transmitter. Due to a faulty lead, the taped programme had to be relayed by a microphone to the transmitter although this led to poorer quality and the invasion of extraneous sound.

The broadcast was made from the kitchen with the VHF aerial trailing from a window. Minutes later, loud intrusive bangings came from the door. The house-holder's wife opened the door and was confronted by a Post Office official and a policeman. The lady was frightened. I came forward and took control. The policeman said that they believed there was an illegal transmission taking place in the house in breach of the Wireless Telegraphy Act and they wished access to the house. There could be no doubt there was a transmission since they could hear it being played in the background.

Because of the noise, which threatened the transmission, and with the consent of our hostess, I agreed to them entering the house to speak in the privacy of the lounge. I advised the officers that we were listening to the programme – which was audibly true - and, in absence of a warrant, denied them access to the kitchen, where the transmitter was. They left. The broadcast continued. RFS operatives did not know at that time that it had been jammed.

We suspected – and we were right - that the police had covered both the front and back of the tenement. There were a few members of Glasgow RFS personnel in the house so, having broken down the aerial system, several left concealing bits and pieces. They included a man and a woman in the guise of a couple who smuggled out the transmitter. By then, RFS had learned that the broadcast had been jammed and, armed with details, a Glasgow associate rushed off to the Express who published the story. So if the broadcast was lost through jamming, there was a consolation of more people knowing of the broadcast than would have actually heard it!

And yet both the GPO and BBC denied jamming. The Express reported, however, that: "Many listeners report noisy interference and some straining enthusiasts hear nothing but a high-pitched throb."

The operators thought the matter was over, but several weeks later, a constable called at my flat with a request that I agree to take part in an identification parade. I assured the constable that I approved of Radio Free Scotland and gave him a briefing on the injustices in political broadcasting visited on Scotland.

Two days later, back in my flat, I received a telephone call from a chief inspector who claimed I had filled the mind of his young constable with nationalist propaganda. He rushed to assure me that the request to appear for identification did not come from the Edinburgh Police but from – and here a tone of disapproval came into his voice – the Glasgow Police. All he wanted to know was, would I participate in the parade? I assured him that I always wished to be of help to the force, but, in this instance, did not believe my participation would serve any useful purpose. And so the conversation concluded amicably.

In a rare humorous moment, the Scots Independent gave a buccaneering account of the "Brigton Affair":

"THE "BUSIES" GET BUSY AT BRIDGETON

The streets of Bridgeton were plastered with posters proclaiming that Radio Free Scotland had prepared an eve of the poll broadcast to the people of Bridgeton. The people themselves were, no doubt, eagerly awaiting this message by the

Scottish National Party candidate.

The TV programme came to a timely end and the introduction to the election broadcast began. Three minutes later the jammers got to work and phut! went the programme, rendered almost inaudible by the staccato sound of the jamming machine. About this time, however, there was feverish activity in and around Bridgeton. Someone in authority had set a trap to catch the "pirates".

Were they successful?   Well, read on. The "pirates", if there were any, were never caught. The transmitter, if there was one, was never found. The householder, from where the broadcast took place, if indeed it ever took place, was never charged. Which is all very confusing! But let me explain, or rather let Jimmy himself, explain the excitement which followed his night at the "Telly".

The Scene – a tenement flat in Bridgeton.

Characters – Wee Jimmy, his wife and a few "freens".

Time – 11.10pm. Wednesday, Eve of Poll. A loud knock on the door.

Jimmy answers – "Hullo. Whit dae ye want."

"We are Special Branch men and we have reason to believe that you are operating an illegal broadcasting equipment on your premises, and we want in to find it."

Jimmy – "Well, yir no' getting' in, see."

SB men – "But we demand to get in."

Jimmy – "Whit wi'oot a warrant, ur ye daft or whit."

The Special Branch men retire to regroup their forces. Two PO radio detection vans draw up at the close. The plot thickens. Meanwhile in other parts of the city, a well-known national political figure is driving home hotly pursued by a squad car full of SB men. They hoped they would catch him red-handed at the broadcast, but no one had told them that it might have been a recorded programme. They reached Kilmarnock and gave up in disgust – foiled again.

Two other party officials are being closely pursued by two pairs of flat feet through the dismal maze of back streets that is Bridgeton's Mile-end. The two suspects board a tram car bound for the Gallowgate. The SB men give up to save some shoe leather.

The Big Black Box

The scene now shifts back to the stairhead of Jimmy's house. The time is now 2am. Something is seen to leave Jimmy's house. It is a big black box, carried by two men gingerly downstairs, past the SB men, and into a waiting car. They suspect something. The car drives off, one PO van in hot pursuit. The big black box is empty.

Two of Jimmy's "freens" leave his "at home" carrying a brown paper parcel past the noses of the remaining SB men, into a waiting car and away at high speed. They suspect nothing. I wonder what was in that parcel.

Next day – the same stairhead. SB knock at Jimmy's door. Jimmy answers.

1st SB man – "What was in that big black box?"

Jimmy – "Whit black box?"

2nd SB man – "We have a warrant to search your house."

Jimmy – "Aw, you didna need to bother, come in an' see ma gramiphone pick-up. Are ye satisfied?"

3rd SB Man – "We're going to charge you."

Jimmy – "Whit's the charge?"

1st SB Man – "Well, no. It's not you we want, it's the Party we want"

Jimmy – "Whit Party? A hid nae party here last night."

2nd SB man – "We mean the National Party."

Jimmy – "Oh, a see. Yis didny jam Lord Haw Haw frae Germany - but yis jammed wur ain boys frae broadcastin' – ur yis feert they ur getting' too strong for yis? Whit is yis onywey, Scots or English or whit?"

All three SB men in chorus – "We're Scots, of course."

Jimmy – "Well, get down that b….. stair and don't come back. Traitors, that's whit ye are, traitors!"

Exit three SB men to regroup their scattered forces for another, perhaps a final assault.

Back in Edinburgh, the GPO brought in detector vans in attempts over several periods to track down the transmitter. It was the equipment and the operators they were after if they were to mount a successful prosecution. For the programme and publicity staff, it was another thing. They were identified publicly and could have been picked up easily – once those who did the actual breaking of the law had been caught in the act. But there were consequences for all. The operators and technicians worked for Ferranti and even if not prosecuted, could have been deemed a security risk and lost their jobs. As a law apprentice, and then a young solicitor working in a prestigious firm of solicitors in Edinburgh, involvement with a pirate radio station would not have advanced my legal career. But such is the impetuosity of youth.

CHAPTER 7

Expansion Westwards

In 1962, there was a by-election in West Lothian. The Scottish National Party obtained a first class result, not winning, but reaching second place on a very healthy share of the vote. It was that election, following closely on the Bridgeton by-election of the year before, that established the SNP as a potential political force to be reckoned with. As candidate, Billy Wolfe, later Chairman of the SNP, did not allow his job as an accountant in industry or his position as a Justice of the Peace, to stand in the way of political progress and he and his team invited Radio Free Scotland to come from Edinburgh and interview him.

After the election, the RFS team was approached by people from West Lothian who, with the blessing of Billy Wolfe, wanted to set up their own station. We helped them get a transmitter and offered to supply them with scripts so that they would not run short of material but, with one important condition, they would keep us informed of what they were doing. It was expected that they would supply copies of their output that would be of interest in Edinburgh. In all other ways, they would operate independently. RFS West Lothian made its first regular broadcast in November 1962.

Pirate radios are unwise to keep records of their illegal activity in case they might be used in evidence in a prosecution. So with the passage of time and people, there is little record of the operations of the West Lothian branch. It appears the station transmitted around the burghs in this large county constituency with some regularity. As West Lothian Constituency Association was one of the most active, innovative and creative organisations in the Scottish National Party, RFS would have found little difficulty in recruiting people to prepare and transmit the programmes. Equally, Billy Wolfe would have been keen to get the social and economic case of the SNP over to his electorate in any way possible.

But as West Lothian's predominant interest lay in fighting elections, it is surmised that radio communication during an election would have been a priority. There was, however, not much coverage of the regular activities of West Lothian Radio Free Scotland in the national press and its output seemed to have been more local in nature than that of the Edinburgh station.

Glasgow was a different matter. It started transmitting in 1961 and was run by David Rollo, who still took a strong interest in his brainchild, and Angus McIntosh, a Glasgow activist who had returned from a stay in London. The programmes were prepared in Angus's flat in St George's Cross and at times, with a casual disregard for security, were transmitted from there. Sheila McIntosh was not married to Angus at the time, but she has related hearing from him how an evening would be allocated for making the programmes. David Rollo would turn up with some scripts. Angus would bring out his notes and they would work together on the texts, before recording the final product.

At other times strict security was followed. One of the engineers was Gerry Bayne who also appeared on programmes as "Denis McKay". His description is more detailed.

"The weekly schedule involved a programme planning meeting and a recording/editing session on a Sunday evening and then the actual broadcast on the Monday evening. Usually we would meet at Angus's home on the Sunday night for recording and on the Monday evening gather again at St George's Cross simply to collect the transmitter etc. and from there travel to a prearranged location – usually a top flat or any house with a clear outlook. But before we arrived at our chosen transmission site we had to allow time to lose the Post Office Detector Van which frequently tailed us as we set off from Angus's home."

Then, describing the early days, he mentioned that they operated with a "Heathkit" self-assembly transmitter and afterwards used a more powerful Hallicrafter machine. He has no recollection of the Effective Radiating Power of any of the transmitters, but assumes that it was modest resulting in very limited coverage and yet, surprisingly, there were some reception reports from a considerable distance away. On the plus side, it meant that their equipment was indeed easily transportable! Gerry mentions that he was handicapped in using his parents' home where he stayed, for trial transmissions. His father was a Sheriff!

The Glasgow programmes were very political in content and were prepared at that stage by a core group of David, Angus, Gerry and Bill Lindsay. Many others contributed. Right at the beginning, they appeared to have crashed. Following the well rehearsed RFS policy of "brazen cheek" they had invited Captain Richard Laning, commander of the Polaris Missile depot ship, Proteus moored in the Holy Loch and his crew to listen in to an anti-missile broadcast, transmitted on behalf of the population of the West of Scotland who faced obliteration in the event of there being a nuclear war. The programme said that innocent people in Scotland were being exploited just as much as those in Latvia or Estonia, under Russian control.

There was good advance publicity in the Mail and Express. The downside was a subsequent report in the Scottish Sunday Express on 12 March 1961 summed up in the headline: **"Pirates Flop with Pirate Broadcast"**, then reporting that not only was the signal too weak but the American television sets had yet to be tuned to UK frequencies. If that were not enough, the American navy men or those not out on the spree in Dunoon or Glasgow would have been tucked up in bed. The following day the Daily Mail ran the story: **"The 'pirate' voice is silent again."**

And then the true story emerged. During both broadcasts - perhaps to avoid any international embarrassment to the US arising from Scottish opposition to Polaris expressed through giant demonstrations and attempted boarding of the American ships by anti-nuclear activists - the BBC had smothered the weaker RFS signal by continuing to transmit its carrier wave at full power. The BBC transmitters were normally switched off a short time after the last programme ended. But, of course, the explanation was in small print while the headlines made the real impact.

We did learn something new from these reports. The Post Office was now maintaining that listeners could be fined for tuning in. No sign of an open society here!

What is true is that of the three stations, Glasgow carried more heavy duty material. For instance in February 1962, there was a very long piece on emigration that would have lasted 15 minutes or so. Very good stuff, but only for the converted or political enthusiasts! It read well in print, but was too long for radio as a medium designed to catch and hold the attention of people who had tuned in by accident or for novelty.

In 1962, Glasgow RFS produced a series of party political broadcasts on behalf of the Scottish National Party in the run up to the local elections and I made an appeal on behalf of the network for branches of the SNP to apply for coverage in their area. With three transmitters, it was possible for a short time to spread our wings and cover localities away from the centres of population. Elections provided the perfect focus for these short bursts of evangelical activity. There was no way our operators could do this on a sustained basis without exhausting themselves by doing too much broadcasting when they had jobs and families to consider. Programming was easier to manage as there would be a set tape with a local add-on – much less work. Also as time progressed, contributions came anonymously from people who worked for the BBC and STV.

Not enough credit has been given to the operators who repaired the transmitters and undertook the risky task of making the broadcasts. Occasionally, they did feature. On 27 September 1962, a Daily Herald feature looked at Radio Free Scotland from their aspect. It had a photograph (whether of the operators or 'models' is a matter of conjecture), but the text read: "An autumn dusk in Edinburgh. Two men in sports jackets carry the complete Radio Free Scotland unit past two policemen as they head for the night's new broadcasting spot. Soon it will be time to go on the air. The simple hand-built apparatus used by the men of Radio Free Scotland is tuned to beam the programme to a potential audience of a million and a half people."

For the first time, their views were recorded. Under the sub-heading: **"Sacrifice"** they related:

"We have actually climbed on a bus and sat next to a policeman with the transmitter on our knees and the radio aerial bent in our hands" said one operator who is a scientific worker. "Now we can pack the lot on the back of a scooter. So long as we operate from a densely populated area of the city and move as soon as the broadcast is finished we think we can elude the GPO."

For the wives who wait at home, the planning, production and broadcasting of the weekly programme means sacrifice. "It takes my husband away from home for nearly 30 hours some weeks," said one wife with a lot of patience and a lot of pride in the broadcast.

"He's concerned with putting the weekly programme on tape and broadcasting it late at night" she revealed. We know that there have been only a few sustained searches for them, but there is always the worry that the police and the GPO men will knock on the door some night. It is a constant strain but none of the wives I know connected with Radio Free Scotland would really want their husbands to haul down the pirate flag."

While it would be very rare in Edinburgh for an operator to prepare the programmes, this was the case more frequently in Glasgow. Still, there was a lot of work. The operators had to locate allies, preferably occupying a top flat, who would be willing to share the risk, prepare a rota so that the transmitter moved from location to location in an irregular manner, convey the equipment to the site, connect and dismantle it, re-transport it and maintain it in workable condition. All this would be on top of the need to take at least one night each week out of their lives for a period of 8 months each year.

In December 1962, Glasgow RFS took responsibility for the next parliamentary by-election – Glasgow Woodside - and received the thanks of candidate Alan Niven whose broadcast had been reported in the Guardian. By the end of the year, RFS had managed to carry out a broadcast on Hogmanay. The programme contained an interview with Mrs. MacDonald, a 30-year old housewife in Bridgeton, whose husband, a fitter in a large engineering works, had just been paid off and was looking for a job.

Her answer to a question as to what they would do if he didn't find work soon, was typical of the age. "It looks as though we'll have to do what my sister and her husband have done – go to Australia where there seems to be plenty of employment in all kinds of work." And when asked whether she wanted to stay in Scotland, her answer was direct, but had a lot of pathos: "We certainly would. All our roots are here, our children are being educated here, and we would prefer them to have a Scottish education. After all, why should we have to emigrate?"

The nationalist movement had serious worries over the level of Scottish emigration and made social and economic comparisons with other countries. One programme in March 1963 focused attention on the state of Scotland's slum housing, especially in Edinburgh. It then contrasted the position in Denmark through the interviewing of Mrs. Vera Stevenson, a Danish lady from West Jutland, then living in Edinburgh. She described how houses were being built in Denmark on a large scale and that the housing queue was only around three months compared to years in Scotland.

Local issues sometimes provided the best return. In August

1963, Glasgow RFS devoted a programme to the Dumbarton "calamity" - the closure of Denny's shipyard. It carried an interview with the SNP Candidate, Alex Gray. Such an important matter would attract a large audience in the area affected by the closure and allowed the SNP to obtain coverage that would otherwise have been scarce. In this case there was the follow up advantage of good reports in the local papers carrying the content of the broadcast to those who had missed it.

By now, by-elections began stoking up pressure on the political establishment. It was manifestly unfair that one political party, the SNP, should be excluded from party political broadcasting. Employing its usual irreverence, RFS wrote to the political parties in the Kinross & West Perth By-election (1963) offering them the opportunity to have their candidates take part in a 20-minute RFS discussion. The invitation was especially addressed to the Tory candidate, Sir Alec Douglas Home who also happened to be Prime Minister seeking validation by election to Westminster! The concept was attractive to the Guardian, Record, Scotsman and the Glasgow Evening Citizen who all covered the story. For the record, the candidates failed to respond and RFS felt free to give time to SNP Chairman and Candidate, Arthur Donaldson.

Glasgow RFS also scored a major hit in December 1963 over an alleged housing scandal involving a former Lord Provost who vehemently and extensively denied the allegations in a substantial article in the Daily Record. In the 1964 General Election, SNP Candidate Dr. David Stevenson in the Glasgow Woodside Constituency appeared on RFS. The broadcast seemed to have been a very informal affair. He turned up at a Glasgow tenement at 9.30pm, for a discussion on content over tea and coffee. He has described how an aerial was 'turfed' out of a window and the broadcast would go out live soon after.

But whether exhaustion had set in or not, press reports relating to RFS, even in the Scots Independent that had faithfully reported progress, became spasmodic. There was an indication that broadcasts may have taken place especially in Glasgow, but by now with the sudden growth too of the Scottish National Party as a major force in Scottish politics, RFS was no longer the only beacon of light and hope it had been.

Things had changed for the better and the attention of most activists was focused more on elections and organisational growth. I had long since become National Secretary of the SNP, campaigning for both legal party political and election broadcasts. Douglas Henderson was involved in training of candidates and activists. It was also true that BBC and ITV had begun to mention the SNP in their news reports and even discuss the subject of independence. By 1966, only Angus McIntosh remained as a regular broadcaster and he, too, was an SNP candidate. The Edinburgh station resumed broadcasting in February 1966. Its last recorded output was in January 1967.

CHAPTER 8

Glasgow Rises Again

Just when everyone had assumed that Radio Free Scotland, like its signal sometimes, had faded into legend, the station revived in Glasgow in the late sixties. By then, the SNP was making a triumphal breakthrough, but some like Angus McIntosh and David Rollo recognised that the Party's base was still insecure and reckoned the advances would be jeopardised by hostile media coverage. In early 1967, (before Winnie Ewing was elected in the Hamilton by-election), an eleven-strong team of Glasgow activists and candidates was assembled. Most of the production section used aliases for their own protection.

Ian Douglas, now an SNP Councillor, has recounted that transmissions were still being made on VHF on 53.25mhz, on the BBC TV frequency, after close-down of the BBC evening service. Two of the team later worked for Radio Clyde in different capacities.

By 1970, the extension of BBC late night services made it more difficult to obtain audiences on the television frequency. Around 1970 to 1971, the team moved on to a medium wave band frequency of 260 metres. With the exception of an election broadcast for the Stirling Burghs by-election in 1971, the medium wave programmes altered radically. Instead of a twenty minute magazine format, the programmes became more ambitious. The standard length was now three hours and the station broadcast on Sundays.

Obviously, music must have played a substantial role as it would have been impossible to script a heavy duty political commentary over that length of time. Either the production team would have collapsed with the fatigue or the audience! Broadcasts went out "live". One script that has survived showed that RFS had become satirical, if not existential, and used short recorded skits, such as:

"My Music

Introductory Music

"And this week's guests in My Music are Sir Alex Douglas Home and Margaret Thatcher against Willie Ross and *[a visiting Northern Irish politician]*.

As usual the first round is Name That Tune and this one is for you, Sir Alec."

Music played "Scotland the Brave". Begins to fade after a short while.

"What? You need to hear a bit more, Sir Alec."

More music played, fades away.

Sir Alec – "Um, ah – It's Scottish, isn't it."

"Well done, Sir Alec, half a point."

"Um – Coming through the Rye?"

"Oh, HARD LUCK, Sir Alec. Just half a point and we'll move on to Willie's tune."

Music played of "There was a lad was born in Kyle."

Fades away. In loud exaggerated Scottish voice.

"Fair Fa your honest sonsie face,
Great chieftain o' the pudding race"

"No. No. Willie, it's not Burns night" – aside "he hasn't been the same since he got some applause on STV last week."

"Well – Ah – half point made and we'll move to Margaret's tune - Margaret put down that bottle (of milk?) and listen."

Sound of straw sucking dry.

Music played. Oriental music. (Slightly drunk voice).

"Ah (hic) Yeas that would be one of your Gaelic Winds – I mean Airs."

Willie Ross in background "You're full of wind yourself."

"How dare you."

"Now Now guests HA HA we're not in the House now. We'll move to our Irish tune."

"What can you make of this?"

Music. "When Irish eyes are smiling".

["Well, as I was saying – You've got two minutes to get out."

"Look! *Look, there's* a bomb – let's get out."]

Noise of scrambling to get out, mainly bottles and cups being knocked over – shouting: "Better wake up the producer." "Save the tea set."

Margaret "Where's my bottle?"

Final music

For one reason or another, this provoked the authorities to action. They swooped. There are three clippings with descriptions. The first one **"Free Scotland radio closed by the police"** from the Daily Express was factual and perfunctory. Another from the Glasgow Herald, **"Swoop on "Radio Free Scotland"** was essentially the same, but with comment from RFS and George Leslie.

It was The Guardian under the by-line of their respected political reporter, John Kerr, which gave the most information. All articles are undated, but there is a note attached stating that RFS was raided on Sunday, 7 May 1972.

Under the heading, **"radio closed in raid"**, John Kerr wrote:

"Radio Free Scotland, the pirate broadcasting station in Glasgow which supports the nationalist cause, was raided and closed yesterday by Post Office officials and police. Post Office officials took a statement from a man and equipment was impounded.

The station had been on the air, on 260 metres, for about an hour broadcasting its usual Sunday afternoon programme of pop, folk and Scottish music, punctuated by occasional political comment, when four Post Office officials and two detectives arrived with a warrant for entry. A week ago, during the Sunday transmission, men were seen with transistor radios and binoculars, outside the tenement flat on the south side of Glasgow where the transmitter had been operating.

Mr. George Leslie, chairman of the Glasgow regional council, who was present when the station was raided yesterday, said: "We will launch an appeal to set RFS back on the air as an effective force in the shortest possible time so that the voice of nationalism can be heard in Scotland."

The lack of radio and television time available to the smaller political parties has always been a sore point with the SNP. As a result, there has been a pirate radio faction within the party for the last twenty years. RFS, known as "Rufus" to its supporters has never been officially recognised by the SNP, but it has always attracted enthusiasm from many of the rank and file of the party.

After a lull in activity following the general election and last year's municipal elections in which the party suffered major defeats at the polls, the Glasgow station started regular broadcasts at Christmas. The object was to encourage new support particularly among young people – hence the emphasis on popular music and the transmission time during Sunday afternoon. On the strength of mail received at the Glasgow regional office of the SNP, the organisers estimated that they had a listening audience of about 10,000."

The article ended by reporting that RFS intended to broadcast from Edinburgh, Dundee, Inverness, Argyll and the Western Isles. Indeed, shortly after, RFS provided a surplus VHF transmitter for Stornoway.

The man arrested was SNP activist, David Murchie who has described what happened:

"I was asked if my house at 32 Leven Street, Pollokshields could be used. I asked what kind of aerial would be required, and was told the longer the better, and horizontal was as good as vertical so Willie Spiers who had provided a good proportion of the recorded folk music for the radio and I fitted an aerial cable to the roof ridge from my house the full 100 metre length of Leven Street. After tests I was told this was the best and most far reaching signal ever achieved.

I was told that normally the location of the equipment was changed after every three to four weeks to try to avoid detection; it was detected at my house on the third week of transmissions. This may have been due to the fact that the reception was so good. The police, radio tracers and special branch raided the house on the late Sunday afternoon and demanded entry. When George Leslie and I asked for a search warrant, they produced one and were allowed in.

When they found the equipment, they demanded to know who owned it and who was responsible for the transmissions. I thought as it was my house that was being used, I was going to be charged anyway so I told them that I alone owned and was responsible for the equipment and transmissions. I gave them a written statement to this effect. After some further questions about where the equipment was purchased, which I refused to answer, they threatened to lock me up if I did not give them this information. I told them to go ahead. What they did not know was at that time I could not have told them if I had wanted to as I did not know. The equipment was then taken by them. I was told I was being charged and was given a receipt for the materials being taken.

At the trial, I was defended by Winnie Ewing. When I asked how I pleaded to the charges, I said guilty on all counts. The judge said that due to the fact I had no previous convictions of any kind, on this occasion, he was going to impose a fine. When asked how I intended to pay the fine or if I wished time to pay, I told the court that I refused to pay and wished no time to pay. Winnie told me that this would result in a custodial sentence. The judge then adjourned the court and said he would reconvene in half an hour. When the court reconvened, the judge said that the fine would be taken by Civil Diligence.

I did not know what this meant. I asked Winnie and she told me this meant that if the fine was not paid in full, a warrant would be made by the court for a sale of any of my assets to the value of the fine.

Winnie said that this was the first time in her experience that a judge had issued this kind of judgment. In this kind of case, they obviously did not want the publicity that Radio Free Scotland and the SNP may have received if I had been jailed. I did not want this kind of action to be taken against me, and asked Winnie to delay things until I discussed the outcome with my wife and then to decide what to do next. Meantime, unknown to me, Yvonne and Mike Murgatroyd, great nationalists who, I am sure, you must also have known, had paid the fine."

On 26 May 1972, the whole Glasgow team moved to Rothesay to cover the SNP Annual Conference. It had been a struggle to get going again after the impounding of the medium wave transmitter. Another transmitter was located at short notice. RFS was on the air again on reduced power! The team occupied a house on a hill in Rothesay and broadcast Conference reports from there. This was done with some success since the Greenock Telegraph reported the following day that the broadcasts were clearly heard over Bute.

Ian Douglas believes that the time-frame for the medium wave transmitter was around 1970-1976/77. Apart from the raid and arrest, other incidents involving the VHF equipment were minor. For example, RFS used a decoy car to take post office investigators on a wild goose chase. On one night near Bellahouston Park in Glasgow, the decoy pulled over. The following vehicle stopped about 100 yards behind. Somebody got out of the car and raised the bonnet as if it had broken down. So one of the lads walked back, introduced himself as a mechanic and offered to repair the car!

On another occasion, after RFS had been primed by the

Scottish Daily Express to broadcast a story that they could then quote, the occupier of the arranged high flat had taken cold feet after everything was set up, forcing the operators into making a mad dash to premises in Renfrew which had a good situation and where the house-holder was more reliable!

CHAPTER 9

Mission Accomplished

Radio Free Scotland was different from Radio Caroline and the other pirate commercial stations. It was not there to sell advertising or to make money. It was not there primarily to sell a message – although that became an integral part of its operation. It started broadcasting because of a well-founded grievance. Its mission was to draw attention to an injustice and give the Scottish nation an opportunity to hear arguments from all parts of the Scots political spectrum and beyond.

It was not a vehicle for the Scottish National Party or any other nationalist organisation. On a number of occasions it offered its facilities to candidates of all political parties fighting elections. That view was shared at times by the SNP. The Party Chairman and Candidate in the Kinross & West Perth by-election in 1963 insisted on RFS inviting other candidates to debate with him before going it alone when there was no take up.

So what was this grievance?

It was a serious one. The nationalist movement did not get any broadcasting time. This was the injustice that impelled the taking of risks. Some like Frank Thomson, Angus McIntosh, Douglas Henderson and I flaunted their own names. Others preferred to use pseudonyms. It wouldn't have saved them if the operators had been caught and the GPO had decided to make a big case of it. After the first two years, there was less chance of that for political reasons as "martyrdom" would have fuelled the already explosive expansion of the Scottish National Party. But in the last years of the Radio, there was the prosecution of David Murchie. So it was not just scaremongering to get publicity.

The case for the illegal broadcasts was set out in a leaflet which, a couple of years into the broadcasts, was printed for distribution to the many people who wrote to the RFS contact address. An extract gives a fair picture of the position.

> "It was in 1955 that the Welsh Broadcasting Council decided to inaugurate a new policy for Welsh broadcasting: a policy which recognised Wales as a country *sui generis* (sic) and allotted to Plaid Cymru, the Welsh National Party, time on the air for party political broadcasting at election and inter-election times.
>
> Accordingly, the four political parties in Wales – Socialist, Conservative, Liberal and Plaid Cymru – were approached by the Council and invited to send their respective representatives to a meeting with the Council. It should be mentioned here that the Council had invoked the power given to them under the terms of the BBC Charter to enable them to put on the air regional party political broadcasts to supplement such broadcasts as were put on air by the BBC in London for the United Kingdom as a whole.
>
> The effect of the Council's invitation to the parties was immediate. From the then Postmaster General, Dr. Charles Hill, came a directive forbidding the Council to proceed further in their

attempt to cater for all shades of Welsh interests."

The aim of Radio Free Scotland was to maintain a high moral tone so that if the authorities acted, they could find themselves in a very embarrassing position, especially since in the wake of the Beveridge Report on Broadcasting, the National Broadcasting Councils of Scotland and Wales had called for "regional" political broadcasting. The UK parties at Westminster had set the rules so that minority political views would not be allowed broadcasting time.

This applied to small British parties, but even more unfairly to the SNP, since the requirement to contest 50 out of Scotland's 71 seats was a huge target. As for Plaid Cymru, the situation was impossible. With only 36 parliamentary constituencies in Wales, the British target of 50 could never be achieved. It was also certain that, were the SNP and Plaid Cymru to join forces, the rules would be changed smartly. In any event, the two parties were so weak that they would have had difficulty in meeting a smaller qualification.

RFS operators faced potentially large fines rather than prison sentences – although those were permitted under the legislation. Although these could have been met by public subscription, one or more might have made a constitutional case of it, refused to pay and gone to jail. The authorities, of course, were not daft so ultimately when there was a conviction the Sheriff instructed that the fine be collected by civil diligence rather than provoke a prison stay if the fine was not paid.

So Radio Free Scotland played "blind man's buff" with the authorities. There is no doubt we were a nuisance and the first reaction was one almost of indignation that we had upset the establishment game. But in the second phase they too played "cat and mouse". For example, the Bridgeton broadcast broke election law and this caused them both to jam the broadcast and seek to gain evidence for a prosecution.

RFS staff could not know when the GPO or its political masters would change tactics, and every now and again there was a scare.

For example, Ian Douglas has recounted that after he had been recording a programme in Glasgow, he left the flat to go to work as he usually did in the late evening. He was carrying an oscilloscope. Because the streets were quiet, he noticed his Hillman Avenger was being followed. He tried to lose them and went on eventually to Yarrow's Yard in Scotstoun, taking it through security. When he finished his work, the car that had been following him had gone. Meantime, the transmission had been taking place from the flat at St. George's Cross. Obviously, RFS Glasgow, unlike Edinburgh, did not take security too seriously – indeed, they may have wished to provoke action!

The 1956 transmitter started up at a time when the nationalist movement was at its lowest ebb. It certainly gave the few of us who were interested in Scottish independence a great boost. For once, the blanket of silence had been lifted. RFS was conceived by David Rollo as a political tool and a device to rack up interest in the SNP – hence its peripatetic existence. By moving around, it was unable to build a regular audience. Being run by few people, it eventually fizzled out.

The Edinburgh operation had a different objective – that of cultivating an audience in one City. It was organised professionally with programmes, publicity and transmission, each having its own role. It had one political advantage not open to the 1956 station.

It started at a time when national sentiment in Scotland was stirring. In 1956, the economy of Scotland was on the cusp of decline. Unemployment had begun its climb and ruinous emigration was soaring. The British Empire, with its prestige and colonial job opportunities, was dying in the aftermath of the abortive attack on Egypt at Suez (1956). By 1960, members in the SNP were organising for growth in a systematic fashion and the Party had begun to eclipse its rivals in the fragmented nationalist movement. The dash and impertinence of RFS encouraged the troops.

While RFS kept to its strategy of involving the various wings in the movement, gradually it gave time for party political broadcasts by a renascent SNP, starved of the broadcasting opportunities which its progress deserved. The SNP did not feature on mainstream TV or radio shows. It was rarely mentioned on news programmes.

Radio Free Scotland in Edinburgh used its 'pirate' credentials to attract audiences and publicity. Despite early equipment failures, it operated on a regular basis and encouraged the emergence of permanent stations in Glasgow and West Lothian.

RFS Edinburgh regularly received around 10 to 31 record requests and answers to quizzes per week which was an excellent return to the RFS "post box" at 16 North St Andrew Street. More importantly, the publicity it received gave hope to the emergent national movement. It also focused attention on the exclusion of the SNP from general broadcasting coverage as well as from the party political and election broadcasts made available to the Labour, Tory and Liberal Parties. This later underpinned a campaign by the SNP for broadcasting rights.

Glasgow RFS showed even more stamina and went on to broadcast for two years after the Edinburgh station ceased and then was active, if intermittently at times, until 1976/77. It had its own character and did not fear to deal with the great political issues of Western Scotland.

For Radio Free Scotland, whether continuing or not, the real victory came in 1964 when the Westminster parties gave way grudgingly. The SNP was allowed to participate in a new series of Scottish election broadcasts and given parity with the other parties in Scotland. Six months later, the ice broke again when the SNP was allocated 5-minutes for its first party political broadcast. From then on, there were further political battles for coverage on a British basis and as has been seen, the injustice re-emerged in critical form over the May 2010 General Election leadership debates when the SNP was excluded. The solution? Perhaps SNP Westminster candidates should become "pirates" again and refuse on principle to pay the licence fee if the SNP is again excluded?

But that is a fight for another generation. Winning the right to have distinctive Scottish broadcasts was victory enough for the generation of "pirates" who had fought the early battles and continued to put pressure on the authorities - for the first allocation was for five minutes only - while the Westminster parties carved up a large chunk of time for themselves. Over the years, constant campaigns produced a fairer share. Without Radio Free Scotland, it is arguable the battle would have been harder and longer.